Animals, Animals!

DO COWS HAVE KITTENS?

A Question and Answer Book about Animal Babies

by
Emily James

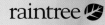
raintree
a Capstone company — publishers for children

Raintree is an imprint of Capstone Global Library Limited, a company incorporated in England and Wales having its registered office at 264 Banbury Road, Oxford, OX2 7DY – Registered company number: 6695582

www.raintree.co.uk

myorders@raintree.co.uk

Edited by Jaclyn Jaycox
Designed by Juliette Peters
Picture research by Jo Miller
Production by Laura Manthe

ISBN 978 1 4747 2791 4
20 19 18 17 16
10 9 8 7 6 5 4 3 2 1

BRITISH LIBRARY CATALOGUING IN PUBLICATION DATA
A full catalogue record for this book is available from the British Library.

PHOTO CREDITS
Getty Images: Photographer's Choice RF/Ronald Wittek, 10; Newscom: Image BROKER/Alexander von Düren, 8 (inset), VWPics/Gerard Lacz, 22; Shutterstock: Andrew Mayovskyy, 27 (top), ANURAK PONGPATIMET, 32, Dudarev Mikhail, cover (cow), Guy J. Sagi, 6, ilozavr, 27 (bottom right), Joseph Scott Photography, 8, Kjuuurs, 12, Maksimilian, 28 (top), njaj, 1, back cover. Oksana Kuzmina, cover (kittens), Orhan Cam, 28 (bottom), Rita Kochmarjova, 18, 20, Savo Ilic, 14, scigelova, 16, smereka, 26, USBFCO, 27 (bottom left), Visun Khankasem, 4, Volt Collection, 24

Design Elements: Shutterstock: irin-k, pale62

Printed in China.

DO COWS HAVE KITTENS?

No! Cats have kittens.

Newborn kittens are born with closed ears and eyes. A kitten's eyes take a few weeks to fully open. A mother cat protects and feeds her kittens.

DO COWS HAVE FAWNS?

No! Deer have fawns.

Fawns are born in the spring. They have reddish coats and white spots on their backs. The spots help fawns blend in with the forest surroundings.

DO COWS HAVE GOSLINGS?

No! Geese have goslings.

Baby geese are born with tiny flaps of skin between their toes. The webbed feet help the goslings paddle and swim.

DO COWS HAVE CUBS?

No! Bears have cubs.

Bear cubs are born in the middle of winter. Little cubs stay with their mother inside a den. In the spring the cubs leave the den for the first time.

DO COWS HAVE JOEYS?

No! Kangaroos have joeys.

pouch

Joeys are about half the size of a grape when they are born. At birth the tiny joeys crawl into their mother's pouch. There they stay safe and warm for many weeks.

DO COWS HAVE TADPOLES?

No! Frogs have tadpoles.

Tadpoles hatch from eggs. They have small, round heads and long tails. They wiggle in the water like little fish. After a while the tadpoles grow legs and become frogs.

DO COWS HAVE FOALS?

No! Horses have foals.

Foals are able to stand an hour or two after they are born. Soon they are jumping and playing. Foals also have a good sense of smell. A foal can find its mother by sniffing for her smell.

DO COWS HAVE KIDS?

No! Goats have kids.

Baby goats are called kids. At birth a kid weighs about 2.7 kilograms (6 pounds). Kids are often born in groups of two or three. A kid drinks milk from its mother until it is eight to 12 weeks old.

DO COWS HAVE PUPPIES?

No! Dogs have puppies.

A group of puppies born at the same time to the same mother is called a litter. A large litter can have 12 or more puppies in it. Puppies in the same litter are called littermates.

DO COWS HAVE LARVAE?

No! Bees have larvae.

pupae

larvae

A newly hatched bee is called a larva. A larva eats a milky fluid, honey and pollen. About 10 days after hatching, the larva spins a cocoon. Inside the cocoon the larva becomes a pupa. About 11 days later, the pupa leaves the cocoon as an adult bee.

DO COWS HAVE CHICKS?

No! Penguins have chicks.

Penguin chicks hatch from eggs. Most chicks are born with a layer of soft feathers called down. These feathers are not waterproof. A chick depends on its parents for food until it can go in the water and hunt on its own.

DO COWS HAVE CALVES?

Yes! Cows have calves.

Calves can stand up and walk soon after they are born. Calves spend time in grassy fields. They follow their mothers as the cows wander and graze.

Animal babies

Some baby animals look like their mothers.

calves   ⟶   cows
fawns   ⟶   deer
foals   ⟶   horses
kids   ⟶   goats

a goat with two kids

Some animals look different from their mothers.

tadpoles   ⟶   frogs
larvae   ⟶   bees

a frog and tadpoles

Some animal babies hatch from eggs.

goslings → geese
chicks → penguins
larvae → bees
tadpoles → frogs

goslings hatching

Some animal babies are born in the open air.

puppies → dogs   cubs → bears
kittens → cats   joeys → kangaroos
kids → goats

a newborn kitten and its mother

GLOSSARY

coat hair or fur on some animals' bodies. Fawns have spotted coats.

cocoon covering made of silky threads. A bee larva makes a cocoon to protect itself while it changes from larva to pupa.

den place where a bear hibernates, such as a cave or hollow tree

down the soft, fluffy feathers of a young bird

graze move about and eat grass and other plants. Cows graze in fields.

hatch break out of a shell. Goslings, tadpoles, larvae and penguin chicks all hatch from eggs.

litter group of baby animals all born at the same time to the same mother

pollen powder made by flowers to help them create new seeds

pouch flap of skin that looks like a pocket in which some animals carry their young

pupa insect at the stage of development between a larva and an adult

webbed having folded skin or tissue between an animal's toes or fingers

COMPREHENSION QUESTIONS

1. Baby kangaroos are called joeys. They stay in their mother's pouch for many weeks after they are born. What is a pouch?

2. Fawns are born with white spots on their coats. Why do they have spots?

3. Which animal baby would you most like to have as a pet? Why?

READ MORE

Animals and Their Babies: Horses and Foals, Annabelle Lynch (Franklin Watts, 2016)

Baby Animals (Young Beginners), Emily Bone (Usborne Publishing, 2016)

Wild Baby Animals (DK Reader), Karen Wallace (Dorling Kindersley, 2012)

WEBSITES

www.animalfactguide.com
Learn amazing facts about animals on this website.

www.bbc.co.uk/education/clips/z92jmp3
This video clip explores how some baby animals look like their parents.

www.kidsdiscover.com/teacherresources/baby-animals-science-lesson
Here you'll find activities to help you learn more about animals.

LOOK FOR ALL THE BOOKS IN THE SERIES

DO COWS HAVE KITTENS?
A Question and Answer Book about Animal Babies

DO GOLDFISH FLY?
A Question and Answer Book about Animal Movements

DO MONKEYS EAT MARSHMALLOWS?
A Question and Answer Book about Animal Diets

DO WHALES HAVE WHISKERS?
A Question and Answer Book about Animal Body Parts

INDEX